SEE YOU SOON, HOLLY JUNE
HOLLY TAKES THE BIG APPLE!

Written By Madison Clark
Illustrated By: Lexie Haugen

© 2023 ALL RIGHTS RESERVED.
Published by She Rises Studios Publishing **www.SheRisesStudios.com**.

No part of this book may be reproduced or transmitted in any form whatsoever, electronic, or mechanical, including photocopying, recording, or by any informational storage or retrieval system without the expressed written, dated and signed permission from the publisher and co-authors.

LIMITS OF LIABILITY/DISCLAIMER OF WARRANTY:

The co-authors and publisher of this book have used their best efforts in preparing this material. While every attempt has been made to verify the information provided in this book, neither the co-authors nor the publisher assumes any responsibility for any errors, omissions, or inaccuracies.

The co-authors and publisher make no representation or warranties with respect to the accuracy, applicability, or completeness of the contents of this book. They disclaim any warranties (expressed or implied), merchantability, or for any purpose. The co-authors and publisher shall in no event be held liable for any loss or other damages, including but not limited to special, incidental, consequential, or other damages.

ISBN: 978-1-960136-11-4

Introduction

Madison Tanner Clark was born and raised in Miami, Arizona where she was a cheerleader by day and a rowdy cowgirl with Labradors by night. Her whole life she wanted out of Arizona and explore the world, only to later come back home! When she was 18, she moved to New York City for her undergraduate in Media, Culture, and the Arts. There she worked as a stage manager for several off-Broadway productions and spent most of her time as a manager at a Wall Street doggy daycare which her own dog daycare, Desert Pups, is inspired by. Desert Pups is now open in Mesa, Arizona where she and Holly currently reside.

Upon graduation, she moved to Las Vegas to go full-throttle in her writing and social media career. Madison also has her own writing company where she helps bloggers, marketing agencies, and influencers with their copy.

Madison has co-authored two other books with She Rises Studios. *Becoming an Unstoppable Woman* where she was open about her struggles with PTSD after witnessing a terrorist attack and *Me Too But Never Again* where she tackled the topic of sexual abused towards minors. *See You Soon Holly June* is her first independently authored book. This book series is based on her own dog, Hollywood June, a Havanese who has helped her through the struggles of her 20s and given her unconditional love in exchange for chicken nuggets.

www.instagram.com/themaddieclark
www.DesertPups.com
bark@desertpups.com

HOLLY

With her long, silky dark hair and really big eyebrows, she makes people smile everywhere she goes.

Tucker is a fluffy, white puppy called a Maltese. He is from Cleveland, Ohio. He tells Holly stories from his puppyhood where he would vacation at the most beautiful resorts in the world and where he gets his super fancy bow ties.

Holly's long wavy ears with faded pink bows start to perk up as Tucker says all his other doggy friends all grew up the same way he did. "They all have new bows? I have had these bows since I was a puppy and he changes his every day?" She starts to freak out a little.

Then Tucker asked Holly about her puppyhood. Holly didn't want to tell him the truth. *What if he doesn't want to be my friend anymore when he finds out I didn't have a puppyhood like him? What if he thinks I'm weird or different for not having nice collars or cool stories? Should she tell him the truth?!*

Tucker stood there with his mouth open. "You lived on an island?! That is so cool! Tell me more, tell me more!" Tucker was bouncing and wagging his tail like crazy, waiting for Holly to continue her story!

"If I can tell you my truth, I was scared to tell you about my puppyhood." Holly was surprised! "Some dogs only pretend to be my fur-end just so they can go on vacation with me or get cool bows as presents. They don't like me just for being Tucker. But you do, Holly."

Even though they were both wagging their tails, Holly felt sad that Tucker thought she would judge him or use him. But wait, isn't that what she thought he would do, too? Not every puppy is as they seem. We all have our stories that make us unique!

"I'm really happy we're friends, Tucker. Do you want to try some Cuban food? I can teach you all about my culture while we eat!" His tail started wagging as he ran in a circle, "I love yummy food! Let's go!"

About the Author

Madison Clark is the owner of her doggy daycare, Desert Pups, as well as a professional copywriter with 8 of experience in both industries. She holds a Bachelors degree in Media, Culture, and the Arts from The King's College in New York City.

Madison is an expert in all things dog-related as well as different works of writing. She has co-written in 2 other books, Becoming an Unstoppable Woman and Me Too But Never Again.

Currently, Madison is busy running her doggy daycare in Mesa, AZ, and is passionate about educating the younger generations through her knowledge of dogs on how we can treat others around us and how to go about different life experiences.

She has published numerous articles and blogs on a plethora of topics ranging from sexual abuse to PTSD where she shares her own stories about resilience and how to ask for help. Through these harsh experiences, she is able to portray these circumstances in ways that are easy to digest with a lesson at the end of it.

In Madison's free time, she enjoys teaching the kids at her church, Living Word Gilbert, and can often be found at Desert Pups or hanging out with her star, Hollywood the Havanes. She welcomes the opportunity to connect with readers and can be reached at bark@desertpups.com.

Overall, Madison brings a wealth of knowledge and expertise to See You Soon Holly June, Holly Takes the Big Apple, and she is excited to share her insights with both children and parents.

Made in United States
North Haven, CT
06 June 2023